THE VERGER
in the Church of England

THE VERGER
in the Church of England

A PRACTICAL GUIDE

JOHN G. CAMPBELL

First published in 1998 by
KEVIN MAYHEW LTD
Rattlesden
Bury St Edmunds
Suffolk IP30 0SZ

The right of John Campbell
to be identified as the author of this work
has been asserted by him in accordance with the
Copyright, Designs and Patents Act 1988.

ISBN 1 84003 231 6
Catalogue No. 1500218

Cover design by Jaquetta Sergeant
Illustrated by Peter Wilks
Printed in Great Britain

CONTENTS

THE AUTHOR

Following a career in hotel management John Campbell began his ministry as a verger at Bradford Cathedral, as bishop's verger. He has since served in Winchester Cathedral as an assistant verger before moving to Carlisle Cathedral to be head verger. At present he is dean's verger of Lincoln Cathedral. A former chairman and general secretary of the Church of England Guild of Vergers, John is currently the Guild's overseas liaison officer.

FOREWORD

The purpose of this book is to provide information to those wishing to know more about the work and world of the verger, whether they be in full- or part-time employ or voluntary. It does not set out to be a comprehensive account of the history and work of the verger.

The remit of any individual verger will vary from church to church. This book hopes to answer as many questions as possible, though inevitably some will remain. Where this is the case, the names and addresses in the final chapter will provide a further source of information. The description of the work of the verger may also be of use to those who employ vergers, and may serve to demonstrate to those who do not, the benefits that the verger can bring to a church or cathedral.

Some of the terms and spellings used within these pages may differ from those familiar to the reader; all are recognised, albeit locally. What is said of churches can equally be said of cathedrals, chapels and in fact of all ecclesiastical buildings. All references to the verger in the masculine are purely to avoid textual clumsiness.

I am indebted to those vergers who have contributed to this book in any way, with thanks to those whose items and ideas have been used and apologies to those whose have not. The aid of Brian Buttery, verger, sacristan and parish clerk of St Wulfram's, Grantham and David Thomas, former head verger of Southwark, Rochester, Grace, San Francisco and Blackburn Cathedrals has been invaluable. Thanks also to KMM for her proof-reading expertise.

THE VERGER'S PRAYER

Almighty Father,
from whom every family
in heaven and on earth is named,
who has called us into the fellowship
of your Church;
grant, we pray,
that in all our parishes
we may fulfil the duties
and enjoy the privileges
of our spiritual homes.
And on those who offer themselves
for service, as verger in the house of God,
bestow the fullness of your grace;
that, united in love
to you and one another,
we may show forth your glory
and hasten the coming of your kingdom.
Through Jesus Christ our Lord.
Amen.

Chapter 1
BACKGROUND AND HISTORICAL INFORMATION

The verger's roots lie deep in history and can be traced back through the medieval Church to the New Testament and beyond. The verger today is someone committed to serving the Lord through practical ministry in the church, whether full-time, part-time, or as a volunteer; someone with purely ceremonial duties or with other church responsibilities as well. The verger serves through a very special, indeed unique, and time-honoured lay ministry.

The ancient office of verger has its beginnings in the earliest days of the Christian Church. The vergers of today often retain many of the duties their various predecessors held. In the fourth and fifth centuries they came under the heading of 'inferior officers of the church'. The *mansionarius*, the housekeeper, and the *ostarius*, the door-keeper, are but two of the forerunners of the verger. Gregory the Great created the office of *custos ecclesiae*, whose duties included the lighting of candles and lamps in the church. The sexton, bedel, sacristan, clerk, parish constable and altarist have all contributed tasks to the duties carried out by the modern-day verger.

The first office-bearers to be chosen by Jesus' twelve apostles, as recorded in Acts chapter 6, were specifically appointed to look after the practical needs of the new fast-growing Christian community, but they were not chosen lightly; men 'full of the Holy Spirit' were selected to carry out these important practical tasks.

Verses 1 and 10 of Psalm 84, known as the verger's psalm, say 'O how lovely is your dwelling place, O Lord God of Hosts . . . I had rather be a doorkeeper in the house of my God, than to dwell in the tents of unrighteousness'. As the psalm suggests, the verger holds one of the oldest-established offices within the church. Vergers were found in temples of Old Testament days as well as in the great churches and cathedrals of medieval times, just as they are in the many different worship centres of today.

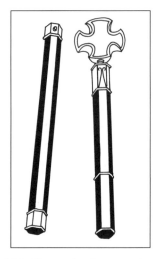

A verge which dismantles for ease of transporting

The verger gets his title from the verge – also known as the rod, staff, mace, wand, or virge – which he carries in procession before a dignitary of a cathedral or parish church. The verger literally made a way through the standing congregation of the medieval church. The term comes from the Latin *virga*, a rod or a twig, which was the origin of the old English spelling of virger. The modern spelling reflects the French *verge*, which comes from the same latin root. The verger, with his rod or twig, turns and inclines to make a way for the procession.

Carrying the verge –
the 'normal' position, at forty-five degrees to the floor

Carrying the verge –
the 'at rest' position, used before a procession begins and when it
comes to a complete halt

The practice of carrying a verge in a procession was popular in medieval times. Often made of wood, among other things it served to keep dogs at bay, or, for those who had the responsibilities of the parish constable, as a truncheon to keep order. By the seventeenth century the wooden verge was replaced by metal or silver versions. A few examples of early verges survive, such as the verge used for the wedding of Mary Tudor to Philip of Spain in 1554, still in use in Winchester Cathedral, whilst a fine example used today at Carlisle Cathedral was used to lead Bishop Oglethorpe at the coronation of Elizabeth I in 1559. The verge used by the dean's verger of Lincoln was made in 1666, the year of the great fire of London. A *twigg* encased in silver, used at Rochester Cathedral, is thought to date back to the eleventh century.

The verge is generally carried in the right hand, pointing forward at approximately forty five degrees. In Bradford Cathedral the verge is carried in this manner for cathedral dignitaries, whilst for those of ecclesiastical rank lower than a canon it is carried resting on the right shoulder. The latter practice is the norm in York Minster.

Carrying the verge –
the 'pause' position, used when there is a pause in a procession

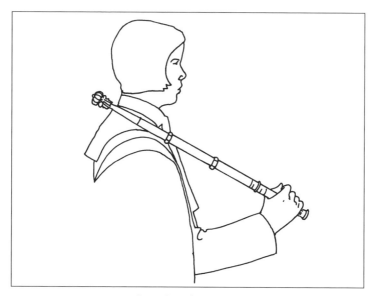

Carrying the verge –
the 'over the shoulder' position, used at some Cathedrals

Chapter 2
THE VERGER'S DRESS

The verger's dress consists of a cassock, gown and a choice of neckwear. The cassock, used widely in today's church, is a useful, though not an historical, part of the verger's uniform. The cassock is basically an undergarment adopted by the verger over which to place the verger's gown, a more authentic part of the verger's insignia.

The gown is more synonymous with the verger. Like most ecclesiastical garments, it would originally have had a practical function, not least as protection from the

The verger's gown with lappets and chevrons

weather; the square collar of today's gown would have been a hood. Primarily an academic gown, it developed for the use of the parish clerk as he went about his work, not only in the church but also in the parish. The lower part of the sleeves, the lappets, were developed to hold scrolls. The chevrons on the sleeves would originally have been ribbons with which to tie small scrolls or documents.

There are many differing forms of neck wear within the church, not least those of the verger. The dog collar, bow tie, tabs and jabot all owe their existence to the cravat and in particular the riding cravat. The eighteenth century parson, the clerk in holy orders and those in lesser orders, for example the parish clerk, all wore cravats which were adapted for ecclesiastical use. Cravats were tied in many and varied ways; some would tie them at the back of the neck, some in a bow at the front, others just let the ends fall on the chest, these variations resulting in the dog collar, jabot, bow tie and preaching bands of today. The most common form of neck wear for the verger is *sub fusc,* that is, winged collar and white bow tie. It is quite incorrect to wear bow tie and preaching bands together.

Neckwear

Jabot

Round neck

Collar and tie

Cravat

Bands

Bow tie

Chapter 3
CEREMONIAL AND PROTOCOL

'Follow Me'. Many have found comfort in these words. Knowing that they will be escorted to the right place at the right time is a privilege enjoyed by cathedral dignitaries, parish clergy, visiting preachers, and others. But who is to decide which is the right place or indeed the right order?

It makes sense that the verger, who is normally a permanent member of staff, should have a general knowledge of protocol for both sacred and secular events. The following suggestions offer a broad look at protocol and can be used in many differing situations, though some local customs may vary. Advice can be sought from places such as mayors' parlours, lieutenancies or even the Lord Chancellor's office. Some situations will have to be tailored to the number of staff or volunteers available.

Seating plans and processional rubrics should be clear and concise, and distributed well in advance to those concerned. These should include any stewards on duty as well as any visiting dignitary.

When dealing with visiting dignitaries it is important that the order of precedence is clear. The representative of the monarch takes precedence in all cases, i.e. the Lord Lieutenant or High Sheriff of a county would take precedence over a town mayor or district chairman. When civic heads are visiting they should be placed in date order according to the granting of their charter, the earliest charter taking precedence. The local mayoral party is always given precedence when other mayoral parties are present. If an event is based on a county, then the chairman of the county council might take precedence over the town mayor. For instance, if an event were organised locally, say by the Lincoln rotary club, then the Mayor would be given pride of place; however, if the event were organised by the Lincolnshire rotary association, then the chairman of the county council would take precedence over the local mayor, should they both be invited.

The following lists are intended to be a general format. It should be noted that the person taking precedence enters last and leaves first.

A civic procession

Lord Lieutenant of the county
High Sheriff of the county
(Local mayor)
(Chairman of county council)
Town mayors
Chairmen of district councils

Should there be a royal presence then clear instruction can be had from the clerk to the lieutenancy of the county.

Suffragan bishops are normally honorary canons of a cathedral and should be included in their number unless they are representing the diocesan bishop. Archdeacons, unless they are residentiary, are also included with the honorary canons; however, outside the cathedral archdeacons take precedence over a dean or provost.

A cathedral procession

(Cross & lights)
(Bedel)
Choir
Verger
Visiting clergy
Visiting dignitaries
Canons emeriti
Verger
(Chapter Cross)
Honorary canons
Residentiary canons
Verger
Dean or Provost
Verger
Bishop
Bishop's chaplain

A parish procession

(Cross & lights)
Choir
Lay readers
Visiting clergy
Visiting dignitaries
Verger
Incumbent
Archdeacons
Churchwardens
Bishop
Bishop's chaplain

Chapter 4
THE MINISTRY OF WELCOME

Vergers seek to enhance people's enjoyment of our churches and cathedrals, to help them appreciate the beauty and significance of the church buildings and their place in history, as well as to share with them the truth of the Church's teaching.

The verger is in the front line of all activities within the church. He is, more often than not, the first or only representative of the church a passing visitor might see; therefore it is important that he be sympathetic to a positive ministry of welcome. After all, one never gets a second chance to make a first impression.

At best, a ministry of welcome includes a team of people ready at any given time (during open hours) to assist the visitor, tourist or pilgrim; or a verger ready to give a word of welcome or lend a listening ear, willing to take time to stop and assist; or even a well-lit warm church with plenty of up-to-date information to hand about the church, its ministry and its activities.

At worst, the visitor is met by a cold dark building with out-of-date notices; or a locked church with a note pinned to the door indicating the whereabouts of the key holder; or a church official busily going about his business without a thought for those who might be on the fringe wanting, or indeed needing, to be noticed and helped; or someone ready to pounce and monopolise the visitors' time, all the while encouraging them towards the offering box.

A visit to a church should be an experience, perhaps a life-changing experience. An old church building is a tangible reminder of the continuity of Christianity, recalling our roots. Visitors may well be either attracted or repelled by what they find. Let the very stones welcome the visitor as much as they can – they have a quiet calming ministry that is as important as any personal approach.

The Church has a ministry to everyone. It makes contact with the regular parishioners with relative ease, but, as an extension of its ministry, needs to be aware of others who may use the building for whatever reason; visitor, tourist, pilgrim, tradesman, the Church has a ministry to them all. One of its aims should be to turn all visitors into pilgrims.

People want or expect to find a church open. Whether they come looking for a house of prayer, a work of art or even a sanctuary from a storm, some sort of welcome is required; having a verger present in the building can only be of benefit to both church and visitor. A locked church, even with a note indicating the whereabouts of the key, presents a negative image. A church that is open, warm and manned, presents an image of care that speaks of the living faith it represents. This is a form of evangelism that should not be overlooked or underestimated, since the church itself can touch people in a unique way.

What are the constituents of a ministry of welcome? First it should be clear that all are indeed welcome. This welcoming atmosphere may be created, as mentioned earlier, by a warm, well-lit church with clear, well-written leaflets, and notice boards which are tidy, not dog-eared, and only display relevant up-to-date information; out-of-date notices suggest an out-of-date message. Posters need to be arresting and eye-catching. Personnel play a large part and really there can be no substitute for a physical presence in the church. The verger and his team should always be ready to talk and to listen and should look tidy, whether in work clothes or ceremonial dress.

An agreed strategy for welcoming visitors is helpful – differing approaches can confuse and annoy the public. For instance, if a visitor arrives while a service is in progress then the verger has a responsibility to give a welcome and to inform the visitor of the options, whether to join in with the activity, sit at the rear for a while and observe or to come back at a later time. To force visitors to participate may be the best way to turn them away, with no hope of return. Likewise, to say at the outset 'There's a service on' and offer no options or explanation may turn the casual visitor into a rejected pilgrim.

Important as a ministry of welcome is, a simple ministry of 'goodbye' can be as effective. In large cathedrals and churches, where it is not always possible to welcome or acknowledge each visitor, a simple greeting by the exit door can convey a positive message. At Lincoln Cathedral, for example, there is a prominently displayed notice which says 'Peace be with you' in fifteen languages on the front, with the Aaronic blessing on the reverse: 'The Lord bless you and keep you. The Lord make his face shine upon you and be gracious unto you. The Lord make his countenance shine upon you and give you his peace.'

Chapter 5
PRACTICAL MATTERS
CARE OF TEXTILES

Whatever the tradition of a given church, it is inevitable that it will house some vestments, robes and altar linen. Whether it be an ancient set of vestments or an everyday cassock and surplice, care should be a high priority, since, with proper care and attention, fabric will last a great deal longer than when treated badly. When worn correctly, garments will look smart and presentable as well as adding to the item's life-expectancy. For instance, wearing a cope incorrectly can put a strain on the fabric and cause weaknesses at bearing points. Wearing a garment correctly is important for, as John Wesley put it, 'Let it be observed, that slovenliness is no part of religion; no text of scripture condemns neatness of apparel. Certainly this is a duty, not a sin. "Cleanliness is, indeed next to godliness".'

Vestries have many functions, one being to store church textiles. The verger may be responsible for the care of many different textiles and fabrics including wool, cotton, linen, and damask. The cleanliness and tidiness of a vestry or robing room is most important. Cupboards should be large enough to hang the garments with plenty of space to allow an air flow, not over-crowded, and tall enough to prevent garments trailing on the floor. If a garment is to be stored in a drawer, as few folds as possible should be used. It is advisable to line the drawer as well as to place a layer of tissue paper (non acidic) over the garment before folding, and to use a roll of tissue in the folds. This will help to reduce the risk of creasing and will act as a rest for heavy embroidery, especially gold work.

Listed below are some of the fabrics commonly used in the church, with instructions for their care and upkeep. Old and very precious vestments and fabrics should only be cleaned, repaired or moth-proofed by a proven expert.

Cotton

Cotton should be washed by machine in hot water. Bleach may be used with white cotton, but only in small quantities and not too often. When ironing delicate pieces press through a muslin; in all cases use a hot iron while the fabric is still damp, or use a steam iron.

Silk damask

Soiled silk damask may be dry-cleaned with dry-cleaning solutions (available under many trade names from large chemists) by gently dabbing with a soft dry cloth. On very delicate fabric turn affected area upside down onto clean blotting paper and apply the solution around the stain from the reverse.

Linen and cotton damask

These may be washed by hand or machine in hot water and may be starched. Iron while still damp on the right side with a medium iron. Linen damask is the more hard-wearing of the two.

Linen

Linen is not only pure and aristocratic, it is also sturdy and long-lasting. With the correct care it will give service for decades, but not if it is treated with strong soaps, detergents and bleaches, which can be disastrous. The best way to care for linen is to wash it in soap flakes, though ivory soap is even better. If it can be avoided, never use bleach; there is nothing better than sunshine (the natural bleach) to restore linen's snow-white effect. It is best to iron linen on the wrong side while still wet, ironing any embroidery first. When storing linen avoid cedar-lined drawers as these tend to yellow the fabric.

Silk
Most silk will lose its shape if washed; it should always be dry-cleaned.

Velvet
Velvet may be steam-cleaned either with a steam press or by ironing through a damp cloth. Dust can be effectively removed by dabbing with a damp cloth. Avoid rubbing. Gentle vacuuming is also recommended. NB. Modern synthetic velvet should never have heat applied to it.

Wool
When washing wool avoid hard water, choose a good soap (as opposed to detergent) and never wash vigorously in hot water.

There are various cleaning problems, which occur more frequently in churches than elsewhere, for which specific guidance is offered below.

Candle wax
If a garment or item of fabric has hot wax dripped on to it this should be left to cool. Never try to wipe it off when still warm. If left to harden for a short while the wax can be peeled off with relative ease. Peel away the excess wax from the fabric by bending the material. Sometimes wax can be eased away with the aid of a knife, but avoid scraping with a knife as there is always the possibility of pressing the wax further into the fabric. Any remaining wax may be removed by placing the affected area between two pieces of blotting paper (or good quality brown paper) and applying a warm iron. For wax spills on altar linen another method is to hold the affected area over a bowl or sink and pour on warm

water, then wash in the normal way. (Trichlorethylene will help to remove stubborn residue.)

Damp
Dampness is a perennial problem. Excess moisture in the air will accelerate the decomposition of most fabrics. Fifty-five per cent humidity is ideal for storing fabrics. If dampness does occur in a vestry, or a particular cupboard, then the affected area should be subjected to gentle heat – never blast with a hot fire or intense heat as this could split wood and cause further damage. Fabrics should also be subjected to a slow gentle heat. For slight problems with damp, and as a precaution against seasonal effects, a small quantity of thymol crystals or silica gel in a drawer or the bottom of a cupboard will help to monitor the situation.

High temperature (direct heat)
All textiles should be protected from high intensive heat. Exposure to extreme heat has a damaging effect, especially on man-made fabrics such as nylon, and also on woollen garments. Even with linen and cotton, care should be taken. When washing in hot water do not boil for too long, as this can weaken the fabric.

Lipstick
To remove lipstick from purificators, wet the item and rub on a small amount of glycerine or glycerine-based soap (such as Pears) over the affected area, set aside for a short while, then wash as normal.

Moth
Two particular breeding grounds for moth are soiled areas of garments (collar and under arms) and fluff. With regard to the latter, frequent vacuuming of vestries and cupboards is essential and will help to control the problem. Any area of a garment at high risk of being

soiled should be laundered regularly, not just prior to main festivals of the Church year. This is particularly important with the amice, ruff, and surplice, which are made of white cloth and easily soiled. Cassocks are another particularly vulnerable item needing care. Whether in constant use or only used once a week, they do become breeding grounds for moth. Moth larvae prefer animal fibres such as wool, silk and fur, rather than vegetable fabrics such as cotton and linen. The introduction of synthetic fabrics in the twentieth century has helped reduce the incidence of this pest. One method of ridding a garment of moth is to place it in an air-tight plastic bag with a small quantity of benzene crystals and leave for a few days, vacuum the garment thoroughly and store in a clean cupboard.

Rust
Moisten the affected area or stain with lemon juice and leave for a short while, without letting the juice dry on the fabric, rinse with water containing a little ammonia, then give a final rinse in clear water before washing as normal.

Scorch marks
Depending on the degree of burn, scorch marks can be removed by brushing with a stiff clothes brush, which removes the burnt end of the fibres.

Ink
Ink may be removed with a mild solution of methylated spirits and hot soft (distilled) water applied as soon as possible.

Wine
A spill of red wine may be removed by applying a little white wine to the area before washing. Rubbing salt on to the stain is another remedy.

Sunlight

Although with fabrics such as white linen, sunlight is to be recommended, other coloured textiles should be protected from the rays of the sun. The ultra-violet content of sunlight can be destructive to textiles and printed materials, in particular synthetic fabrics such as nylon and polyester.

Tar (soot from candles)

Treat as for removing residue of wax, then soak a small piece of cotton in a little lighter fuel, and rub into stain working in from the outside towards the centre. If the stain is small then use a dabbing motion. Avoid spreading the stain outwards at all costs. An alternative to lighter fuel is eucalyptus oil.

Dust

From time to time vestments may need to be vacuumed to release any dust caught in the weave. When these vestments are in a delicate condition, or contain gold couching or any embroidery, it is advisable to vacuum through a piece of muslin. To do this it is helpful to construct a square wooden frame (about 10" x 10"), stretch over a piece of muslin and staple to the frame. Vacuuming through this will prevent any loose fabric or gold work being lost.

The Sacristan in the Church of England, details of which appear in Appendix 1, gives much useful advice which has deliberately not been repeated here.

Chapter 6
PRACTICAL MATTERS
CARE OF METALS AND WOODWORK

Although most churches have a team of willing hands to help, the verger may well be responsible for the cleaning of the church's communion vessels and the brasswork, and for the upkeep of the interior, including the pews, lectern and choir stalls.

Precious metals
Most communion vessels are made of solid silver, silver-gilt, silver plate or are electroplated; very rarely are they made of gold. Pewter was used for a time, and can still be found. Simple definitions of these terms are as follows:
- Silver-gilt – silver covered with a fine layer of gold.
- Silver plate – a base metal, often copper, covered with a fine layer of silver.
- Electroplated – the plating of a base metal by electrolysis.
- Pewter – an alloy of tin and copper (sometimes lead).
Gold, silver and silver-gilt will be hallmarked showing the date, place and name of manufacture.

In the care and maintenance of precious metals the use of any form of abrasive should be avoided at all costs, especially on gold plate and gilt. Washing in soap and warm (not hot) water should be sufficient to keep vessels in regular use in good condition. The occasional use of an impregnated polishing cloth may liven up an item. If a piece of silver becomes particularly marked then the use of a silver soap/paste will restore the silver without undue abrasion. Any item cleaned with water should be well-drained and dried. Draining is best done by placing the item on a dry cloth which will protect the rim of chalices and aid with the soaking-up process. An item with open fretwork or prominent decoration will benefit from the use of a hair dryer to remove any lingering moisture. Items not in regular use are best stored in a cool, dark, dry place, preferably wrapped in a cloth or placed in a specially prepared silver bag. Rubber should not come into contact with silver; *never polish silver wearing rubber gloves.*

Brass
The essence of cleaning brass is to have clean dust-free cloths. As with the care of precious metals, the least possible pressure should be exercised. Using a pad of cotton wool and a reputable brass cleaner is the safest way to achieve a good result. Wearing rubber gloves will protect the hands from excessive staining whilst avoiding leaving fingerprints on the polished article. When polishing fine work, engraving or pieces with angles and crevices it is essential to use a soft brush to enable crevices to be cleaned out. Dried and hardened polish is unsightly and should be avoided at all costs. Pieces with signs of corrosion can be washed in a solution of washing soda before being rubbed down and polished.

The lacquering of brass is not uncommon, but find out which items are lacquered and take care not to polish them.

Bronze
Bronze should not be polished, though a coat of a good quality furniture polish (bees wax) will add a protective patina. Again, avoid allowing the polish to enter fine engraving and turn white. A soft brush should clear any residue of polish.

Woodwork

Well cared-for woodwork, whether furniture or fittings, will look welcoming and inviting. Lacklustre woodwork does not suggest a well-cared for environment and can become a breeding place for beetles and other infestations.

Dusting is an essential part of wood care, although wood will not be preserved by this alone. Regular dusting is the first step to good wood care. Furniture kept up against a wall should be pulled out regularly and vacuumed behind.

A warm damp cloth, soaked in a solution of vinegar and water, will often be sufficient to remove dirt adhering to a polished surface. The wood should be wiped with a clean dry cloth after the use of any water.

The regular use of polish will keep wood both preserved and presentable. The use of paste polishes should be well controlled. As with silver and brass, should the polish dry and be allowed to build up in carving then this will look unsightly and take time to remedy.

Glass

Glass or crystal cruets should be washed out regularly to avoid a build-up of residue. A good practice is to alternate the use of the cruet i.e. use a cruet for wine one week and for water the next; this will prevent any build-up of residue between any particular pair of cruets. Should the inside of glass cruets become difficult to clean, then the use of a little 'Steradent' will prove beneficial.

Chapter 7
SANCTUARY REQUISITES

Candles
Candles should be stored in a cool dry place, preferably in a fire-proof container such as a metal chest, or in a store well away from areas of high fire risk, for example. organ chambers, electricity switch boards.

Guttering is mainly caused by draughts. There are three practical ways of preventing this;
- The placing of caps to the candle will protect the wick from the draught and help pairs of candles to burn down in equal lengths. If caps are to be used then they should be kept clean – dirty, soot-covered caps are unsightly.

- In extreme cases, candles may be placed in a freezer for a short while before use, which will prevent guttering and extend the life of the candle. This is a particularly good practice in very hot weather.

- If draughts are a persistent problem then the use of moulded rather than 'dipped' candles should be considered. Dipped candles hold a certain amount of air between the layers of wax which only adds to the problem of guttering and rapid burn-down.

Wicks should be trimmed regularly – the shorter the wick, the less heat is generated and the longer the candle will last.

The lighting of candles, whether for communion or a daily office, should start with the lighting of the south candles (the epistle side) nearest the cross, then the north (the gospel side). These should be extinguished in reverse order starting with the north standard. The altar gospel candle should not be left to burn alone. Candles placed on retables or riddels should also be lit in this order.

When candles are to be lit ceremonially, as part of the liturgy – for example, the lighting of the Paschal candle on Easter Eve – the use of methylated spirits will help the candle to light easily. Simply dip the wick three or four times in the spirit (letting it dry between dips) and this will help the flame take first time.

The Paschal candle, lit as part of the Easter ceremonies on Easter Eve, should stand alight, during all services, on the north side of the sanctuary until the Gospel is read on Ascension Day or Pentecost, according to tradition. For the rest of the year it can be placed, unlit, by the font as a symbol of the new light received at baptism. During a service of baptism the Paschal candle is lit and from it the baptismal candles are lit. It is in order, in some traditions, to have the Paschal candle standing at the head of a coffin at a funeral. When in use, the Paschal candle should be the first candle to be lit and the last to be extinguished.

Unbleached candles are often used for funerals and in some churches during Lent.

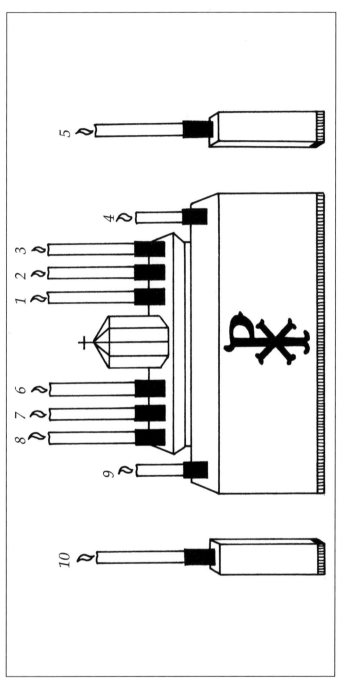

The order of lighting of candles

Wafers and wine
Wafers, or communion bread, like any other food, should be kept in a cool, clean, dry place, not just in a box lying around in the vestry. A large air-tight container will help keep wafers crisp and fresh. Avoid bulk buying; a regular supply throughout the year will alleviate the storage problem and ensure that the wafers are always fresh. Like any wine, communion wine should be kept in a cool dark place. Stock should be used in rotation.

Chapter 8
HEALTH, SAFETY AND SECURITY

Comprehensive regulations are now in force regarding health and safety at work. It is advisable to have a person appointed to this responsibility, who could well be the verger. However, whether or not the verger is officially responsible for the health and safety policy of his church, he does have a general and legal commitment to provide a safe environment not only for the public, but safe also for other staff and the verger himself.

The regulations regarding the 'control of substances hazardous to health' (COSH) should be strictly observed, and all cleaning materials, chemicals, oil, incense, correction fluids used and stored correctly.

Security of a building and its contents can be a headache, though common sense and good housekeeping can help ease potential problems. Valuables should be tied down or alarmed; if in doubt, lock them away. It is easy to concentrate only on small items, such as crosses and candle sticks, when considering security within the church, but much larger items are just as vulnerable. In Passion week 1995 I had a large oriental rug stolen from a chapel in the middle of the morning. There is a ready market for many of the items housed in church buildings. All valuables should be marked and secured to deter potential thieves.

Advice relating to health and safety, fire and crime prevention, performing licences, can all be obtained locally: see your library for information.

Chapter 9
ADMINISTRATION

Where registers and archives are concerned, the duties of the verger are often merged with those of the sacristan and the parish clerk. The following section is included for those whose duties include those of the parish clerk.

Archives
There may be an enormous amount of archive material in a church: paper, plans, books, photographs all need to be taken care of, whether ancient or current.

Some parishes will have all their records safely stored in the church, while other parishes will have some of them lodged in the county or diocesan registry. It is important that, wherever archives are stored, a catalogue of all material is maintained and kept up-to-date.

Storage
Any storage area should be secure, fireproof and clean. The use of thermohygrographs, humidifiers and acid-free storage boxes is recommended. Advice is available from your local county archive office.

Old registers and books need special care. Leather bound books should, at intervals of about five years, be given a very light dressing with a soft cloth using a book-dressing oil, available from library suppliers. Books handled regularly and with care may receive sufficient natural moisture to maintain suppleness.

Books kept on display should never be left open on a flat surface. A V-shaped cradle should be used, or two pieces of wedge-shaped foam to create a cushion. This will help prevent the spine of the book from cracking. Rolls of

Honour and pages of other books which are on display and used often should not be handled; for page turning the use of a spill is advised.

Active worm damage may be remedied by placing the volume in a plastic bag with a gauze pack of an anti-moth agent, such as chlorinated benzene, for about a week. Ordinary naphthalene is not effective.

Tape should never be used to repair torn documents. Starch paste should be used with a narrow strip of fibre sheet, again obtainable from library suppliers.

REGISTERS – OCCASIONAL OFFICES

Banns
Banns take the form of an oral notice, given in a parish on three successive Sundays, stating the intention of a couple to marry. Banns, once read, should be entered in the banns register as having been read. Where a couple live in separate parishes then the banns must be read in each parish. A verger with parish clerk responsibilities must see that the register is kept up to date. Each reading should be recorded and signed and, where necessary, a certificate issued against payment of the appropriate fee.

Baptism
It is a legal requirement that an inhabitant of any particular parish may be baptised within that parish. This is also true for those cathedrals which have parish status (normally those which are governed by a provost rather than a dean and chapter). Where baptism is requested by a person living in another parish, permission should be sought from the incumbent of the domiciliary parish. A baptism register contains a permanent record of all baptised in that church. Those

baptised at the time of their confirmation should not be forgotten.

Burials

Anyone living in a parish is entitled to be buried in the parish churchyard, if it is still open, unless the parish council has ruled otherwise. It is necessary to have a registrar's certificate allowing a burial to take place. After the burial the appropriate portions of the certificate should be completed and returned to the registrar. A burial register should be kept, showing details of all burials in the churchyard, with a plan of the churchyard to indicate each burial plot's location.

Burial of cremated remains

Areas set aside in parishes for the burial of cremated remains should be provided by faculty and are regulated by rules issued by the chancellor of the diocese. As with burials, a plan of the area should be kept and stored with the certificate of cremation issued by the crematorium.

Confirmation registers

These should record the full names and addresses of each candidate. If a confirmation is carried out in another church, then the register is taken and signed by the officiating bishop. A confirmation return form should be completed and handed to the bishop.

Electoral roll

A new roll is required every six years, and needs to be updated regularly to ensure that it gives an accurate picture of a parish's membership. Additions and deletions are often the responsibility of the verger whose duties include those of the parish clerk.

MARRIAGES

The marriage register

However a marriage is conducted in each individual church, the marriage register must be completed in accordance with the rules required by the Registrar General. Each marriage must be recorded as follows:

- in duplicate in the registers supplied which must be completed at the same time;
- in indelible black ink;
- each register must be signed by the two parties, the officiating minister and by at least two witnesses. NB. Signatures of the couple and the witnesses should be made in full, initials should not be used;
- errors which are discovered during the signing of registers should be noted in the margin of the page; these should be numbered and initialed.

Marriage certificates

A copy of the entry in the marriage register should be supplied to the couple in the form of a certificate, as supplied by the Registrar General. This must be a complete copy and include any errors or corrections made.

Marriage licence

Where a marriage cannot proceed by banns, either a common licence or an archbishop's licence should be sought. This is more common in non-parish church cathedrals, but can occur within the parishes, for example if neither party is resident in the parish in which the couple hope to marry.

Marriage returns

Under the Marriage Act of 1949 the incumbent of each church licensed for marriages must supply the local district registrar with a quarterly return showing each marriage solomnised during the previous quarter. If no marriages have taken place, then a nil return should be made.

ACCOUNTS

All monies passing through any cathedral or church must be accounted for in an agreed fashion. Collections, fees and donations should be recorded in the appropriate register and paid into the authorised accounts. It is advisable that this procedure also be adopted for cash which may subsequently be passed on as a donation to a third party. Donations and fees should always be receipted.

Handling of monies
An agreed system for counting money should be formulated, which might include:
- Cash should be counted by two people. Where staffing permits, this should be any two people from a team of three or four.
- Cash counted and banked should be entered in the appropriate ledger immediately.
- Endeavour to vary the times and the route by which cash is taken to the bank. Night safe bags are convenient for the deposit of large sums of money not covered by insurers. A cash collection service is available from most banking establishments for those who have a large amount to deal with regularly.

Chapter 10
CRISIS MINISTRY

As has previously been said, the verger tends to be the first point of contact for everything and everyone that comes to the church. Most things can be prepared for, but the unexpected should be anticipated where possible. With this in mind a customary could usefully be compiled, listing agencies that may be needed in a crisis. Below is a suggested list of headings:

Churches and spiritual help
Legal advice
Financial and benefits advice
Destitution and homelessness
Family and relationship issues
Illness and substance abuse
The elderly
Children and young people
Counselling and trauma
Hospitals and clinics
Christian listeners
Police, local government and DSS.

What constitutes a crisis situation? The bereaved, the down-and-out looking for help, the confused, the bullied child and the battered wife, all these and more may turn to the Church for help. Having information for referral at hand eases the situation. Apart from these personal crises the Church should also be ready to respond to the wider crises and disasters that may occur, whether local, national, or indeed international. Coping with large numbers of people in distress is not unusual. The Lockerbie disaster, the Dunblane killings and the sudden death of Diana, Princess of Wales, are examples of major national events which required great sensitivity to provide for the huge numbers of mourners. Mundane details, such as adequate numbers of votive candles, books of condolence, finding places of peace and quiet for counselling all need to be addressed quickly and efficiently; a prepared customary, listing possible suppliers and agencies, can help to keep things running smoothly in times of crisis.

Appendix 1
WHERE TO FIND FURTHER HELP

For further reading:
The Sacristan in the Church of England – A practical guide
Thomas J D Robertson
published by Kevin Mayhew Ltd.

Ecclesiastical suppliers:
Kevin Mayhew Limited
Rattlesden
Bury St Edmunds
Suffolk
IP30 0SZ

Guild of Vergers – General information:
The General Secretary
14 Pennington Court
245 Rotherhithe Street
London
SE16 1FT

Guild of Vergers – Training course:
The Training Officer
26a Grove Road
Walthamstow
London
E17 9BN

The Church of England Guild of Vergers

Founded 1932
Presidents: The Archbishops of Canterbury and York

Objects:
The Church of England Guild of Vergers is a fellowship in Christ, seeking concord amongst its brethren. It exists to assist us to appreciate the spiritual nature of our vocation and ministry as a verger in the House of God.

Corporate Communion and other services are arranged in geographical areas and dioceses.

No link exists between the Guild and Trade Unionism whatsoever.

Aims:
Local branches arrange various meetings, lectures and social activities which are aimed at stimulating individuals and in fostering an interest in the gamut of the work of a verger, resulting in competent service to the Church.

On a national level the Annual Conference, usually held at a university or conference centre for a week shortly after Easter, has proved to be the focal point of the yearly calendar. Training ranges from fabric management to the laying out of vestments, including knowledge of liturgical movement during worship. This is a unique opportunity for fellowship, learning and relaxation within a well-balanced programme.

In recent years efforts have been made to link the conference with the Guild training scheme, which is open to all members of the Guild. Details of the training scheme are available from the Registrar.

Assistance and advice is available upon request to vergers requiring new posts and to incumbents wishing to appoint a verger.

Administration:
The Church of England Guild of Vergers is administered by the Central Council and consists of the Chairman, General Secretary, National Treasurer, Guild Chaplin, Magazine Editor, Liaison Officer, Training Officer, Conference Secretary and elected officers from the geographical areas throughout the country.

All vergers serving in both cathedrals and parish churches are invited to join the Guild; members of churches engaged in similar work to that of a verger are invited to become associate members. There is an annual subscription which includes six copies of the *Virger* magazine. There is also a local branch subscription.

The Guild shop is administerd by the General Secretary from whom badges, ties and other items may be purchased.

Further information and membership application forms are available from:
The General Secretary
Church of England Guild of Vergers
14 Pennington Court
245 Rotherhithe Street
London
SE16 1FT